Words of an Earth-bound Misfit

Words of an Earth-bound Misfit

Poems by Fatma Naqvi

Woven Words Publishers OPC Pvt. Ltd.

Registered Office:

Vill: Raipur, P.O: Raipur Paschimbar,

Dist: Purba Midnapore, Pin: 721401,

West Bengal, India.

www.wovenwordspublishers.net

Email: editor@wovenwordspublishers.net

First published by Woven Words Publishers OPC Pvt. Ltd., 2017

POETRY

ISBN 13: 978-93-86897-08-4

ISBN 10: 9386897083

Price: $6 USD/ ₹100 INR

Printed and bound in India

DEDICATION

To, all those people who cannot express their feelings and are therefore called emotionless.

To, all those people who'd rather stay silent and be called arrogant than being involved in everything happening around.

&

To, Myself!

ACKNOWLEDGEMENT

I would like to thank my Mother and Father for always supporting me to pursue my dream of becoming a writer.

I would also like to mention my bestie Nilisha, who has forever been encouraging me to write and submit my write-ups to publishing houses. Also, I'm extremely thankful to my English teachers in school because of whom I developed such love for Literature.

And, most importantly I would thank the team of the Woven Words Publishing House for giving a newbie like me the opportunity to showcase my talent on such a huge platform.

I would also like to thank all those people who are proud of me!!

Last but not the least I thank myself for becoming better with each thing I write.

THEM

They are you,

They are me,

Just people from a

Different ethnicity.

They are white,

They are black,

Just people with a

Different quantity of melanin.

They are rich,

They are poor,

Just people with an

Unequal share of wealth.

They are short,

They are tall,

Just people with a

Fatma Naqvi

Different pool of genes.

They are girls,

They are boys,

Just people with a

Different type of chromosome.

They are straight,

They are gay,

Just people with a

Different preference for company.

THEY

We celebrate Birth,

They celebrate Death…

We celebrate Health,

They celebrate Sickness…

We celebrate Graduation,

They celebrate Detention…

We celebrate Union,

They celebrate Divorce…

We celebrate Peace,

They celebrate War…

We are the Commoners,

They are the Rulers…!!!

Fatma Naqvi

WHAT YOU WANTED

Deep down you always knew,

That I wasn't the one for you...

Yet, you lied and fed

My heart with poisoned blood.

You always knew,

That I didn't have the key to your rusted heart.

Yet, you compelled me to

Remove the rust with my blood.

You knew the moment you saw my soul,

That it didn't call out to yours.

Yet, you forced me to tear myself apart.

This was all you did

To not break my heart –

But, oh!!

The irony...!!

You ended up doing exactly that!!

So, please…

The next girl you see

Make sure she wants to be

With You...

For You…

Whole heartedly...!!

Fatma Naqvi

WITH A BLURRY EYE

Sitting by the windy window,

Adoring the weather with a blurry eye…

Inhaling the breathed out vapour

Of the heated romance between the rain and the
Earth – a smell to die for…

Feeling the kiss of the drops as they fall on my
face,

Sending the thrills of joy through my body and
brain…

The gusts of wind blowing my hair as they pass
by,

Telling me to love nature as long as I happen to
live my life…

With a blurry eye,

I sit and see the increasing greenery in the nature
nearby…!!!

SEARCHING MY SOUL

No matter for how long I sleep,

My soul

Still needs You

Like a dry desert longing for rain.

No matter how long I sleep,

My heart,

Still needs You

As much as a writer needs his pen!!

No matter for how long I sleep,

My life,

Still needs You

As the body needs its soul!!

Fatma Naqvi

SILLY GAME

She believed it to be a silly game.

She thought it was just for fun,

Or, merry making!!

But for them,

It was a real game.

A game which defined life and death!!

For them- a war game.

She played the game for their sake,

To make them happy.

They asked her to play the game.

Because her playing it,

Meant life for them…

She thought they loved her,

More than their petty game.

But they, broke her trust

As the game was valued more than her.

At last they won their lives

And she lost her faith in friendship!!

They failed to realize, losing in game is better
than lost friendship!

Fatma Naqvi

SMILE

The word itself is enough,

to brighten up your face.

It brings joy from within

And, hides scars!!

No matter what the situation is,

A smile can provide relief to your soul.

A smile heals, even the most broken hearts,

It is like a silver halo to the evilest of us!!

And your smile,

My dear friend…

Is like a rope, helping me emerge from the dark

Without a single bruise…!!

SOLITUDE

Never thought I'd be so alone,

In the company of people, yet so isolated…

The darkness filled me up,

Light, failed to penetrate my conscious…

My hopes, lost in plutonian shore,

And, goodness forgot to cross my way…

I am filled with despair,

Not knowing where to go…

The world mocks like some hungry whale,

Ready to engulf me now…

Soul-less, I'm moving now

To an unknown destination.

But I'm moving on!!!

Fatma Naqvi

STUPID HEART

Listen here, you stupid heart!

Why do you open up for everyone so fast?

And break yourself like broken shards!

You will survive the breaking a million times,

Because you are immortal, you won't die

And 'Love' won't ever die,

For Love is heart and Heart – Love,

Every time you get a bruise,

My brain closes a part of my soul,

As is the rule.

So, please take care of yourself

'Cause I don't want to lose my soul

For things are beyond my control…!!

SUICIDE

He saw everything happen in front of his eyes.

When He was a kid,

He saw his friend's mutilation happen before of his eyes.

When He was a teen,

He witnessed the bully, torture of the kids in front of his eyes.

When He got a job,

He witnessed his colleague getting harassed by the boss.

When He thought He was finally happy,

He eye- witnessed the murder of his wife.

In the end,

Fatma Naqvi

He witnessed all the worst memories play in front of his eyes,

One. Last. Time

Before committing Suicide…!!

REALITY

Before they turned three,

They thought, life was all play and no work!!

Before they turned fifteen,

They thought, Boards were just another exam!!

Before they turned eighteen,

They thought, Heart-breaks were over-rated!!

Before they turned twenty-two,

They thought, the world wasn't as cruel as
people portrayed!!

Before they turned forty,

They thought, raising a family was a piece of
cake!!

Before they turned sixty,

Fatma Naqvi

They thought, life post-retirement meant
freedom!!

Before they were on their death-bed,

They thought, they were immortals!!

YOU, MY FIRST

You were my first confession,

You were my first lie.

You were my first smile,

You were my first tear.

You were my first laugh,

You were my first cry.

You were my first late night text,

You were my first early morning
disappointment.

You were my first heartfelt happiness,

And, You were my first heartbreak.

You were my first love,

You were my first betrayal.

Fatma Naqvi

But above all,

You were my first confidant,

But, now you are nothing but a mere
acquaintance…!!

FIRST TIME

The first time we met,

Wasn't something ideal!!

The first and the last time we texted

Was totally awkward as well!!

Then my friend went all sort of crazy on you,

And, that was that!!

Any other time we saw each other,

It was kind of clunky for me.

Don't know if I was even noticed by you!!

Gradually the years passed... And now,

That I see you

After a couple of years,

My views about you have gracefully changed...

And so much that

Fatma Naqvi

I might actually like you!!

But you would not know or realize

And deep inside me I'd crave for your love.

HER STORY

Her story, might not be new,

But, it is her story.

The pains she had endured, might be less

But, she suffered it.

The love she got, might not be

love at all,

But, she absorbed it.

The fears she had, might not be unheard of

But, she faced them.

The courage she had, might not be a lot,

But, she had it.

The modesty she possessed, might not be
enough,

27

But, she saved it.

The talent she had, might not be unique,

But, she showed it.

Her end, might not be famous,

But, her life was always talked about.

LIFE-A WHIRLPOOL OF FEELINGS

Life is a whirlpool of feelings,

Feelings-good or bad, sweet or bitter.

Feelings-which bring back thousands of
memories,

Memories of childhood and teenage years.

Memories- about the days spent with friends and
family,

That leave a big fat smile on our faces.

A smile-which instills in us

Many bitter sweet incidences from our life.

Incidences-the bitter ones fill us with rage,

Sweet ones make us feel the happiest person on
Earth.

And Earth- is our life,

29

Fatma Naqvi

A life full of feelings.

CHILD'S VIEW

Sitting idly without the worries of the world,
The children sit and stare out of the window.

Not knowing what the world holds for them,
Wrapped up in the cocoon of love and care.

Without envy and jealousy clouding their minds,
They skip happily about and round.

Loving one and all,
No matter who is what!!

Fatma Naqvi

COMPLETE

Never in my life,

Have I ever felt so complete!!

There was always something that felt
incomplete…

There was always a feeling of loneliness

Deep down within me…

No matter what I did,

It always felt absurd!!

There was a feeling

Like a cyclone was building up in my soul

Ready to destroy my very foundations…!!

All my preparations,

For a beautiful future

Felt insufficient in reality!!

But the day I felt you

I saw my future within my reach…

The day you won my trust,

I gained enough confidence

To transform my thoughts into reality…

And every time you came to me

I knew all my imperfect, matchless pieces,

Have found their place.

Completing me –

Making me Whole!!

Fatma Naqvi

DREAMLESS NIGHT

The days are dull,

And so is my mood.

No sunlight penetrating through

The thick black sky.

Just like my sullen thoughts.

Only, few drops of rain falling,

From morn till eve.

Just like the train of sad thoughts in peace.

The days are unending,

Like the dreams, chasing me in slumber…

It's been long, I'm waiting

For a ray of light.

Like my soul and body for a dreamless night!!

FAKE FRIENDSHIP

In this cruel world of fake friendships,

It's hard to be that faithful friend,

When people around you,

Call you an imposter.

In this cruel world of fake friendships,

It's tough to be a sincere friend,

When everyone is expecting you

To back stab any minute.

In this cruel world of fake friendships,

It's a challenge to be a true friend,

When your friends themselves,

Are waiting to either push you down

Or be pushed down themselves…!!!

Fatma Naqvi

FANTASY FAIRYTALE

You are somebody,

I'll never forget.

You are somebody,

I'll love to spend my life with!!

Talking to you,

Is like enjoying the morning breeze.

Being with you,

Is like a sunset scene!!

Thinking about you,

Is like the fluttering of butterflies.

Missing you,

Is like a moonless night!!

Words of an Earth-bound Misfit

You are like a herb for my pains,

You are like a soothing music,

To my most tiring days!!

Time spent with you is never in vain,

Because, in those moments

I sail in my most beautiful

Fairytales!

Fatma Naqvi

PASSION

She wanted to study Literature,

They taught her science.

She wanted to delve in mysteries and romance,

They pushed her into formulae and algorithms.

She wanted to write for herself,

They made her write for passing exams.

She wanted to collect books,

They made her collect degrees.

Alas,

She buried herself under broken dreams,

And they wrote poetry for her grave!!

PEN AND PAPER

Many-a-times, I sit with pen
And let my heart blot on the paper.

I write about painful moments –
That left everlasting bruises on me.

I write about betrayal –
The feeling which once was foreign but now is
near to my broken soul.

I write about the happy moments –
Which God has bestowed on me.
These moments are like diamonds to me,
because their sparkle brightens my path.

Other times, I just sit and think,
Because at times the feelings are too much to
write.

Fatma Naqvi

Words seem insignificant to describe the beauty,
the strength, and the memories.

So, I let the paper be blank.

And the pen unused.

Instead relive every moment once!!!

LONG TIME

It's been a long time,

Since, I picked my pen to ink my emotions and
thoughts on paper.

That's because,

It's been long since, I felt a thing –

I've been a skeleton far too long.

The emotions and thoughts have so long been
caged now, they don't know how to react.

The feelings are all dormant,

I don't know, whether to smile or to cry.

The world keeps on moving,

Not bothered about the tornado brewing within
me.

That's because, on the surface

I am as calm as still waters,

Fatma Naqvi

but people often forget, there is always an eerie
calm before a storm begins.

I don't know when the cage within me will
shatter to pieces,

Or will just keep on growing,

Until I'm the victim in the cage.

ESCAPE

Writing is an escape,

Escape from the burdens of the world,

Escape from the duties thrust upon you,

Escape from those dreams which will never be
achieved.

It's an escape from memories –

too painful to remember,

An escape from the sins committed,

An escape from the hurt endured,

An escape from hiding the bruises you
desperately want to show.

It's not just an escape from the surroundings,

It's an escape from cleaning up after creating the
mess,

It's an escape from starting from scratch,

It's an escape from the Black Hole you
created....

Fatma Naqvi

THE BLACK HOLE

There are moments in life,

When you feel too lonely to live,

You feel as if you don't belong to anywhere.

It feels as if your soul has abandoned you,

And you're just a hollow body –

A shell of what you used to be!!

There is nothing new or for that matter,

Nothing old which you are used to as well!!

There is simply a void left...

Devoid of feelings...

There is nothing present,

Just You suspended in space...

The void is so huge,

It's like the Black Hole,

Sucking in every light, that was ever yours!!

Returning just darkness, suffocating you

Till, you breathe your last!!!

Fatma Naqvi

STARES

The stares of people haunting me,

Every night like a nightmare...

People said, "Cover up, girl you won't be stared
at then..."

So, I did...

I covered up myself, from head to toe...

Hoping against hope, that I won't be stared at
now!!

But, I was!!

People still stared at me...

I could not fathom the reason of their hawk-like
stares!!

Now, people said, "Why are you covered
entirely, it's a disgrace to your beauty...and
hence, you are being stared at!!"

I was confused at their views...

Yet...I partially covered myself...

Covering my face, I moved about...!!

But, again I was stared at!!

My body was being scrutinized, as if I was an element in an experiment...

Fed-up of being stared and being judged,

I let myself be shown to the world...

As I wanted...

Not caring in the least about the stares, of bigoted people!!

Fatma Naqvi

SUFFOCATION

I am a bird kept in a cage.

Every time I try to fly,

My wings get caught in the wire

And get destroyed!!

Every time I see a bird,

Up in the sky

I feel a longing so strong,

To spread my wings and take flight!!

Every time a little bird,

Opens her wings and learns to fly,

My eyes tear up,

From the lack of such simple joy!!

It's been so long now,

And, even if I was set free,

I'm sure I'd be unable to

Ruffle my feathers!!

I know now,

That it was my fate.

No matter what I try,

I'll live and die in this very cage!!

Fatma Naqvi

I JUST WANTED YOU

I don't know,

What it is to be with you.

I don't know,

What it would feel to be in your arms.

I don't know,

What it would feel if you smiled at me.

I don't know,

How I would react if you cuddled with me on the bed.

I don't know,

What I would do if, you showed me off to you friends.

Because…

I never wanted to be with you!!

I never tried to feel the warmth of your arms…

Words of an Earth-bound Misfit

I never imagined you smiling at me!!

I never thought of any reaction…

Because…

I knew you'd never cuddle me.

I never dreamt being showed off to your
friends…

Because

You wanted the fame and the money,

You wanted the name and the popularity!!

But instead,

I wanted the peace and the love,

I wanted the care and the privacy!!

I just wanted You!!

Fatma Naqvi

AFTER HIM

After Him ...I thought, "No more serious
likeness towards anyone"

And even if I would like someone I'll never say
a word. Wait for them to say it first...

But, yet again I've said it first...

And met with dreams worse than those before!!

I pride myself on not crying over petty issues...

But here I am unable to release the tears...

Getting suffocated as whole...!!

Now I'd rather cry a river...

Than thinking everything again a million times
... Analyzing. Try to think where it all went
wrong!!

Even when I should not like you anymore...

I still do!

Because it's something I can't get rid of so
easily!

I'm the one apologizing here...

When you were the one who...

Said things to make me think of something more...When there definitely wasn't anything at all!!!

Fatma Naqvi

YOU AND I

After yesterday I thought I'd not wait anymore...
Not wait for your messages,
Not wait for you to see my status story.

I won't wait for you...
Not wait for your Good morning text,
Not wait for your, "I'll take care of you."

After yesterday I thought I'd not wait anymore...
Not wait for your movie comparisons,
Not wait for your special emoji's.

I won't wait for you.
Not wait for you to understand me,
Not wait for you to clarify your hints.

Because I understood that,
There were no underlying hints at all.

There was nothing the movie references.

They were just words you said.

But even now...

I've checked countless times if you've seen my status story,

Or, maybe sent a "Hello" text.

But,

I know I'll get stronger through this ordeal.

I won't become a stalker!

I'll just see you smiling once more and Let You Go!!

Fatma Naqvi

MISS YOU

My dear,

It's been so long since we last had any communication. No calls, no texts!!

Yes, it's true that I miss you-a lot!

I wish we were friends still. I don't know what changed? Whether it was you, or me or maybe the circumstances that changed.

But, no matter what, I wish and dearly hope that we can rebuild the friendship without forming any knot.

I miss the 'almost' late night texts.

I miss those explanations that I had to give when you couldn't understand a line or an abbreviation I used!

I miss us teasing each other and the funny references and name calling.

I miss giving a bit of a reality check when your optimism was peak high!

Words of an Earth-bound Misfit

I miss scolding you, when you left conversations
all of a sudden returning back after hours.

I miss our special emoji fights...

I miss all this because-

The almost late night talks gave me a happy
sleep.

The explanations provoked me to write harder,
better things.

The teasing helped soothe my mood.

The reality checks made sure to keep me sane.

The scolding's to make sure you'd never leave
me!!

But, well, nothing matters now...

Because you still left it all!!

I want to explain the things again and be the Yin
to your Yang forever and always!

'Coz I value our friendship a lot and poured my
soul to it!!

Fatma Naqvi

So, it wasn't just the heart that was involved but
my entire soul!!

-Miss You!!

BLOCK

Solitude is what I crave,

Silence feeling like my home.

Because, that is all I'll have in my grave...

Darkness is my armor,

It is all that I have.

Because, it is my only safe harbor...

The shady corner in the room,

Is where I'll be.

Because, there is nothing in me to groom...

I'm the one who is alone,

Always near the door.

Because, now I'm no human just a clone...

Always in my thoughts,

People call me a day dreamer.

Fatma Naqvi

Little do they know, I'm in fact trying to block
them out!!!

BLISS

I had dreams,

I had hopes,

I had aspirations,

I had an aim,

An ambition to fulfil.

But, I never had support.

I had the urge to prove myself for me.

But, I lacked confidence.

Instead, of doing what I wanted to,

I was forced to do the things other's said.

Never, was I given an option.

I never had choice.

The way my life was supposed to turn out,

Was all planned before I was even born.

Fatma Naqvi

As years passed, my hopes shattered.

All the thoughts of proving myself,

Drowned by their decisions.

But, then one day I realized,

I had God.

The Most Powerful.

The One who hears all!!

And then, I let go,

Instead of depending on humans,

I sought after him.

And, He helped.

Fulfilling my wishes,

My ambitions,

Giving me utter satisfaction.

Pure Bliss!!